LIFE BEYOND
— THE —
GAME

LIFE BEYOND THE GAME

A **BLUEPRINT** FOR **ATHLETES** TO IMPACT, LEVERAGE, & MONETIZE THEIR PLATFORM & BRAND

DR. DETRA JOHNSON

Copyright © 2023 by Forward Movement Sports Consultants
Cover Design: Wild Eagle Graphic Design Studio
Published by: 20/20 Living Inc.

All rights reserved. No part of this publication may be reproduced, used, performed, stored in a retrieval system, or transmitted in any form or by any means, electronic, mechanical, photocopying, recording, or otherwise, without the prior written permission of the author Detra Johnson, if living, except for critical articles or reviews.

If you want to purchase bulk copies of Life Beyond the Game, contact us at: www. www.fmsportsconsultants.com or direct your inquiries to dr.djohnson23@gmail.com

1st edition, March 2023
ISBN-13: 978-0-578-76843-4
Printed in the United States of America

This book is dedicated to my parents,
Louis and Shirley Johnson,
my sister-in-law Rosalind McLeod, and
aunt Elizabeth (Jean) Corbitt.

CONTENTS

Foreword. ix
Introduction xiii

Chapter 1	What Fuels Your Passion and Purpose 1
Chapter 2	Shifting from a Fixed to a Growth Mindset 7
Chapter 3	Leverage and Monetize Your Current Platform and Brand 19
Chapter 4	Accept and Embrace the Process 29
Chapter 5	Your Foundation Presence in Communities . . .33
Chapter 6	Career Development and the Business 39
Chapter 7	Entrepreneurship 45
Chapter 8	Know Your Worth 51
Chapter 9	The Value of Having a Mentor 57
Chapter 10	The Art of Networking 63
Chapter 11	Plan Forward. 69
Chapter 12	Mental Toughness. 75

Conclusion 81
Acknowledgments 85
About The Author. 89

FOREWORD
Life Beyond The Game

I moved to the Philadelphia area in 1996 right after the Philadelphia Seventy-Sixers selected Reebok's new signature shoe athlete and global star, *Allen Iverson*, as the #1 pick in the 1996 NBA Draft. During this time, I worked for Reebok as the Global Vice-President of Marketing and General Manager of the Allen Iverson Brand. Currently, I am working as the President of Think450 for the National Basketball Players Association, the NBPA.

I first met Dr. Detra Johnson back in the mid-'90s when she was just beginning her journey working with athletes and attending Sixers games. I was instantly impressed with the manner in which she established herself as a real force within the athlete marketing and brand building fields. She always possessed a kind persistence in her demeanor and a thirst for knowledge which I am sure was her chief motivator in successfully accomplishing her doctorate degree. Dr. Detra has always had a tenacity and resourcefulness about her with respect to helping athletes and entertainers to achieve their desires off the field, as well as, leverage their personal brands for positive change in the community. I am not surprised that her professional journey has culminated in her creating a strategic blueprint for athletes, entertainers, and influencers to follow in their quest to build personal brands that have local, national, and global impact.

Life Beyond The Game, provides years of hands-on and in-the-trenches experiences and insights working with athletes and entertainers throughout their life cycles. Dr. Detra Johnson has seen the good, bad, and ugly as it relates to the careers and post-careers of athletes and entertainers. She has taken her extensive knowledge and put it into a practical and simple resource guide for athletes to strategically create a successful career beyond the game. In my daily work with athletes, I am always asked about *"what"* should athletes be doing and thinking about to achieve success beyond their playing days in building out their personal brands. In the past, I have responded with a personal philosophy, that I have coined:

The Achievement of *"SuCCCCCess"* with 5 C's:

- Commercialization – ideas that generate revenue and grow the business
- Customer – know your audience & improve the customer journey
- Content – focus on the yearning for diverse & authentic storytelling
- Culture – leverage your influence as a trend-setter & trend-validator
- Community – amplify purpose & drive impact locally, nationally, and globally

But now, thanks to the authentic and relevant insights of Dr. Detra Johnson, I can actually couple my *"what"* athletes should be doing with Dr. Detra's *"how"* to do it with her essential step-by-step roadmap. It is very encouraging to know that I now have a valuable and timely resource that I can offer to athletes in, *Life Beyond The Game.* This book is sure to provide an easy to follow blueprint that will enable athletes of all kinds to build, network, and amplify their off the court passions, interests, and future endeavors into meaningful, memorable, and measurable success.

—Que Gaskins

INTRODUCTION

Do you remember the last time you said yes without thinking about it, and you said yes immediately? What were the results of that? Is it something you ended up later regretting? Or was it something you were thankful for? In my case, I am thankful that I was in that moment when my mentor Leah Wilcox, Vice President for the National Basketball Association Commissioner's Office Liasion, asked me if I wanted to be a manager and supervise different areas at the NBA All-Star Weekend. My answer was "*YES*!" It allowed me the opportunity to network and experience firsthand what it took to work in the sports industry. For a few years, I could not wait to get that call so I could be in the mix of the fast-moving, thrilling weekend. But there was one All-Star weekend that stood out the most to me. It was when I met my favorite athlete of all time. I was in complete awe and unsure what to do when this happened.

He was walking off the court and me and my cousin, Vanessa Dawson, were right behind him. We were so close to him - just an arm's length. I turned to my cousin and said, "There he is!" We could not believe it. He was all we had talked about meeting. I am pretty sure our world stopped quickly when he turned around and said something to us. I kept thinking, here we are, and thank God for having the best mentor ever who allowed me to be here. He was all everyone wanted to meet or see. Yes! It was the *CHAMP* who had 6 Rings and played for the Bulls - the one and only Michael Jordan.

The fact that I had access to athletes and entertainers in one place was overwhelming yet exciting. In addition, because I had VIP access, I moved around a lot, meeting as many athletes and entertainers as possible. This was definitely an experience I will never forget.

During that time, I was DJ Jazzy Jeff's personal assistant. I had the job one could only dream about. It was Jeff who introduced me to Leah and several athletes. I remember being in the studio, and Jeff asked me to go and pick up his friend. When he told me who it was, I was so nervous. I asked my brother Carvin Haggins, Grammy Award Winner, to go with me. We pulled into the hotel, and Penny Hardaway was waiting for us. He got in the car, and off we went to the studio. At that time, Penny was in every commercial there was. He was #1 for Orlando Magic. From that day forward, we became friends and every time he was in Philly, he gave me tickets to the game, and then we hung out afterward. When I think about Penny, I look at how he leveraged his platform when he became the head men's basketball coach at the University of Memphis.

It was those experiences I enjoyed the most. And after working at the NBA All-Star Weekend, I truly fell in love with sports, which was pivotal and my initial introduction to the sports industry. Being from Philly, we have so many great athletes, but at that moment, it was all about Allen Iverson. After attending the Sixers games and watching him play, I knew I wanted to work with athletes because of the excitement and energy he created in the city. After expressing my interest in working with athletes, it was then that I was introduced to Heavyweight Boxer Michael Grant and Michael "Big Mike" Harris, and from there it was history.

Working with athletes, I quickly learned how to leverage my platform through my extensive network and social connections. Those connections allowed me to showcase my talent by planning and facilitating Celebrity Weekends for athletes' foundations which took at least eight months to ensure success. It was fun, and thank you, Walt Reeder Jr. (Big Bloc Entertainment) for booking all the entertainers to support such a great cause. That led me to become a publicist and strategic brand marketing specialist for several NFL players, such as Bobby Taylor, Hollis Thomas, Lamar Campbell, Allen Aldridge Jr., Richard "Dirt" Jordan, and WNBA player Rhonda Mapp, to name a few. I also was provided the unique opportunity to be a consultant for the Professional Football Players Mothers Association, Nike, Reebok, and Adidas. I remained grateful and humbled when working with this fantastic group.

The most memorable and rewarding work was with the player's foundations bringing awareness to causes they were passionate about while raising money for children and families in underserved communities. This was an AHA moment for me. I witnessed firsthand the impact athletes had on children when I saw the smiles on their faces when we visited the hospitals and schools or participated in events in the communities. I was in awe. Their platform was huge, and I wanted to do more.

While this is the most memorable and rewarding, the most defeating and unbeknownst to them, is once the athlete no longer is playing, or got traded, those additional resources and that community support ended. In hindsight, I believe many athletes did not realize their foundations could have been operable in that community even when they played for a different team or retired. Some athletes needed to learn to sustain and grow their foundation but continued to leverage their platform to make a difference wherever they played.

I recently conversed with a few athletes who shared their individual struggles after playing. It was extremely hard for them to find their footing and voice after they were no longer in the spotlight. I asked each one of them for one piece of advice to give to current athletes who may not see the importance of preparing for the future, especially if they just got to the league. Hands down, each of them stated they would emphasize the importance of preparing for the future while playing and not when they stop. It is essential to be wise in how they spend and invest their money.

After those conversations with them, I started researching, and it was alarming to find out that *60 percent* of NBA players go broke within five years after leaving the league. In addition, *78 percent* of NFL players are financially distressed within two years post-retirement.

According to the information acquired, several contributing factors supported why many athletes had no choice but to file for bankruptcy. Some of those factors include needing to learn how to manage their money, lack of preparedness, and needing help understanding how to capitalize on multiple streams of income that were not considered risky or bad investments. The stress of not knowing which way to turn was very overwhelming and stressful, especially when they stopped playing. The impact it had on the athlete was exhausting, considering the amount of responsibility they had. The fear of the unknown was challenging, and during those uncertain times, some of them became depressed.

Overall, the average professional athlete's salary received will continue for a few years. Statistics show NBA players' average length in the league is about *4.6 years*. The NFL is even shorter at around *3.3 years,* and the MLB is *5.6 years*. Playing in the league forever is not the case which eventually becomes a reality. This inevitability can have an emotional toll on athletes during the transitional phase, which can be devastating and debilitating, all at one time.

As a sports management consultant and brand marketing specialist, I felt compelled to write this book after I truly realized how many athletes struggle with preparing for the future and finding their VOICE via their platform or brand while playing. The goal of this book is to empower athletes by providing them with practical strategies and tactical tools on how to pivot when ready, from playing to life beyond the game.

Athletes who find the *power of their voice* learn how to leverage their platform and brand, grow their foundation or business, and cultivate strategic partnerships that generate multiple income streams. For example: over the years, Deion Sanders has demonstrated just that. I remember the first time I met him. It was at a celebrity basketball game in Dallas. He was the coach, and I was his assistant. It was fun, and even then, he exerted positive energy and good leadership, and because of that, our team won. It was not surprising to learn that he later became the co-founder of a charter school, a former head football coach at Jackson State, an HBCU, and the head coach at Colorado University. In addition, he made history by being the third black coach at CU. His presence on social media has been impactful and inspiring for many who follow him. Those athletes like Deion Sanders are better equipped and prepared to move forward. They are able to have a new beginning without being financially distressed and the need to fully change their lifestyle. They are able to embrace their new identity by feeling more prepared and confident in a new environment. Even if the change is abrupt, the foundation has been laid, and the transition can be more fluid. This is why I am so excited to bring this information to you. Because the impact athletes can have after their playing days are over can supersede or equally be just as impactful, and that is what we are going to dive into in the rest of the book so let's get started.

CHAPTER ONE

What Fuels Your Passion and Purpose

"If you can't figure out your purpose, figure out your passion. For your passion will lead you right into your purpose."
—Bishop TD Jakes

What fuels your passion and purpose? Have you really sat down and thought about what you are passionate about other than sports? You know what I am talking about. Passion is that strong feeling, emotion, or desire that continuously drives and motivates you to try new things you would not usually try. Did you know that passion is the manifestation of your dreams? It is the ultimate feeling you have when you go to work every day, doing something you are extremely passionate about, and it does not feel like work. You are excited; nothing and nobody can keep you away. Passion is like the old saying, "An athlete cannot run with money in his pockets. He must run with hope in his/her heart and dreams in his/her head." —Author Unknown.

When you align your passion with your purpose, it is an experience you will never forget. However, passion and purpose are not the same. Purpose defines who you are, what you stand for, and your values and beliefs. It is being open to doing more. It is what you were called to do and share with the world. It should be the catalyst you need to reach a large number of people via your platform.

Passion and purpose together will provide you the fuel and lessons needed to stay focused and overcome any barriers you face personally and professionally. Redefining your passion reflects where you are currently in your life. As you evolve, the things you were once passionate about may be different. At this point, give yourself permission to be passionate about other things. Sports do not limit you from continuously walking into your purpose. If anything, you constantly evolve until you fully understand who you are. In the future, you will not be the same version of the current you. Therefore, It is common to re-evaluate the things you are passionate about. In fact, it is necessary.

The perfect time to test the waters and explore is while you are playing. Trust what you are feeling and follow your intuition. Passion is the motivation that drives you to step out of your comfort zone and try new things. Do not be surprised if you come across something you like and now it is at the top of your list. It fuels your passion and keeps you going even when all your energy is depleted.

I remember reading the Zig Ziglar quote "when you catch a glimpse of your potential, that's when passion is born." Can you think of anything you are passionate about and have always wanted to try? It could be acting, writing a book, being a professional speaker, or working in Corporate America as an executive or entrepreneur? The passion you possess can be your reality. As you know, the sky has no limits. Remember, there are an endless amount of opportunities right in front of you. Reach out and grab them and never look back.

Can you think about some athletes who have pivoted successfully because they explored different opportunities? Let us look at Magic Johnson, for example. He looked at one of the needs in urban communities and invested in movie theaters where many of the "Magic Johnson Theaters." Being able to go to the movies in urban communities was monumental and a shift in mindset for many. Dak Prescott learned his motivational speeches had value and trademarked all of them. Steph Curry wrote children's books and started a book club for his fans. Lebron James opened IPromise Charter School and transitional housing for women and children, just to name a few of the community-based initiatives he's explored.

Kevin Durant has an Afterschool center, ownership in Philadelphia Union, and an investment firm, just to name a few. How about Colin Kaepernick, who made a name for himself, not just for being a good quarterback, but for his stance on social injustice. After such an abrupt change in his life, years later, he is now on the Medium board of directors and Inks partnership publishing deals. Maya Moore, amongst other players, leveraged her platform to support social justice and inequality. In addition, two former NFL players, Patrick Hill, a nurse, and Dr. Myron Rolle, a neurosurgeon resident, stood out because they decided to leave the game and follow their passion for living in their purpose. And Troy Vincent, who was inducted into the NFL Hall of Fame and is currently the Executive Vice President of Football Operations for the NFL. Two great athletes from my alma mater, Temple University, are head coaches. Aaron McKie for the Owls men's basketball team and Dawn Staley for the University of South Carolina women's basketball team. She is also an American Basketball Hall of Fame player and coach.

As an athlete, your desire to make it to the professional level had to be all you thought about, just like Kobe. I recall one of Kobe's interviews when he talked about when he was a little boy, and all he thought about was his basketball. How passionate he was about making the shot. I love how he wrote a series of children's books, but that one, in particular, talked about if you are passionate about something you should follow your passion and dreams. Kobe continued to pursue his passion and became one of the most profound players in sports. He never stopped exploring other opportunities that came his way.

Without needing to say too much, another great player who demonstrated that same type of passion on and off the court is Michael Jordan. Air Jordan. Need I say more? He has invested in several car dealerships, restaurants, sports teams, and now Nascar. In addition, Shaquille O'Neal who invested in Google, Papa John's, Auntie Annie's, car washes, Five Guys, 24-hour Fitness, and Krispy Kremes. He is a funny commentator on ESPN and in the commercials he's featured in.

Passion and energy are what these two sisters, Venus and Serena Williams, bring to the game every time they step foot on the tennis court. They are so much fun to watch when they play. But the amount of time and dedication they needed to make it to the next level is incredible. Venus has an interior design and clothing company. Serena has a venture capital firm, fashion line, management company, and pro sports team.

Naomi Osaka was one to watch after she fully opened up about her struggle with mental health. She was not afraid to speak her truth and advocate for herself, but she became a role model for other athletes who felt comfortable talking about what they were mentally going through. As a result, she started a powerful movement considering everything that was happening in the world.

Last but not least was the power move former Atlanta Dream player Renee Montgomery made when she became one of the owners of the Dream team. She fought for diversity, equity, and inclusion in the WNBA and created her own lane and seat at the owners' table. That move opened the door for many other women to walk through.

The moral of the story is that when you follow what you are passionate about, it aids in self-development and self-improvement. You are proud of your accomplishments towards your goals, whether big or small. Your passion is often aligned with whatever career you explore that will eventually provide a sustainable income. When you feel a part of something that matters to you, you tend to invest a lot of time and effort into it. Even when you encounter challenges, you learn how to be resilient in problem-solving skills and more strategic in making more valuable decisions. Begin to self-reflect and figure out ways to adapt to the ongoing changes and new environment.

The goal is not to be complacent during the self-development phase. Roy E. Disney once said, "when your values are clear to you, making decisions becomes easier." You must take the steps needed to acquire information by researching the area you are interested in. The goal is to stay knowledgeable and current with everything. Networking is crucial when engaging and surrounding yourself with veterans in the field who can help you effectively navigate this process while improving your skills.

Once you understand the importance of adding value to your actions, you will become more deliberate with your moves as you learn from others. One thing you know is that being flexible and embracing the process should motivate you to keep going. Your grit and zest will continue to drive you to learn about trends in that field, putting you at an advantage to be successful as you shift to a growth mindset. I challenge you to do the following:

- Identify 3 areas of interest you are passionate about or would like to explore?
- Who do you know who is currently working in that area?
- Do you have any contacts in that area who can help you connect with others who work in that area?

CHAPTER TWO
Shifting from a Fixed to a Growth Mindset

*"Once your mindset changes, everything on
the outside will change along with it."
—Steve Maraboli.*

Athletes have a vast platform that can open many doors without hesitation. Once those doors are open, you must change your mindset, be flexible, and open yourself to exploring new opportunities. How you think and what you believe impacts every aspect of your life. What you think about the most is what keeps you going. I remember reading this quote, which stuck out to me, "We become what we think about. Energy flows where attention goes." ~Law of Attraction. When you are focused, it is easy to concentrate on the one thing that drives and inspires you. As an athlete, you are often driven by grit, motivation, determination, and achieving that one goal to win.

Therefore, you are extremely disciplined and committed to crafting your skills. The time and energy you dedicate to studying films and learning plays take patience and analytical skills. You have been conditioned over many years to work hard and never give up, no matter how challenging it gets. The fact that you have to always be mentally prepared for the unknown makes you more aware of your surroundings.

Do you remember the moment you heard this? "Welcome to the league!" Then shortly after, you started hearing from current and retired athletes about how to prepare for life beyond the game. I remember watching an interview when a reporter asked Marshawn Lynch what advice he would give to young players in the league, and he said, "Take care of y'all bread, so when y'all done, you can go ahead and take care of yourself." Lynch went on to talk about living outside of your means and always thinking about the long game. Focus on the now but prepare for the future. Having the right people around you who can help you grow and learn how to generate multiple sources of income is essential, ultimately positioning you to successfully move forward. It was a great interview and the gems he dropped were powerful, and for many athletes, relatable.

I remember when Allen Iverson was playing for the Sixers, he was one of the most-watched and sought-after athletes. Even though I was in awe of him and his mad skills on the court, it was actually his representative from Reebok, Que Gaskins, who fascinated me the most. Que always had Allen's best interest at heart. He was so positive and great at brand marketing and advertising. I enjoyed conversing with him. He taught me how to navigate through the sports industry. He always made time to answer my questions and provided support whenever I needed it. Que focused on the long game and how to position yourself for the future. He added value to those he interacted with by empowering athletes to be prepared, not just while they were playing, but for when everything ended.

It can be challenging to think beyond what is right in front of you. I challenge you to take the first step by thinking outside the box and visualizing what your life would look like if you were not an athlete. Now is a good time to start exploring your options and find out what you are passionate about other than your current job. This requires you to change from the old way of thinking focused on crafting your skill, to preparing yourself to shift to a new skill. This will expand your knowledge while you learn about new careers. You begin to have opportunities, skills, and qualifications needed to pursue that career path which is when you start to shift from a fixed mindset, just focusing on being a professional athlete, to having a growth mindset, where you are now exploring different things.

Shifting the mindset requires you to think at a new level, which is also called multidimensional. According to Carol Dweck, "In a growth mindset, people believe that their most basic abilities can be developed through dedication and hard work - brains and talent are just the starting point. This creates a love of learning and resilience essential for great accomplishment." You begin to remind yourself that you are more than just an athlete and then give yourself permission to do more than one thing at a time, such as being a student, businessman, or woman.

Therefore, no matter what you decide to do, adding to what you know or learning a new skill will be necessary. If you want to work in sports in some capacity, align yourself with the right people who can teach and give you the tools needed to grow. The people in your circle should add value to you and vice versa. If they cannot add value to you, are they worth your time, energy, and attention? One of the most complex decisions you will have to make is the possibility of eliminating anyone who may cause you stress or anxiety. You do not need to add stress. You have enough on your plate; at this point, you just need to focus on the positives.

As an athlete, the feeling of anxiety can quickly start to rise when you only focus on one skill. This may make you feel trapped, wondering if you have the tools you need to have when it is time to pivot from playing. I challenge you to start exploring different things you like and research as much as possible to prepare you for the next level.

Think about it this way. You are currently using 10% of your brain as an athlete. The goal is to shift to using 70%, which will move you from a *linear* way of thinking (from point A - getting drafted - to point B - becoming a professional player). To a *multidimensional* level of thinking (being a professional player and doing other things while playing, such as becoming a business owner, coach, or doing an internship at your favorite company).

Do not underestimate the power of reading to expand your mind during your free time. What you read can be a great strategy to start a conversation with people you are trying to connect with. Your ongoing research should determine who you need to have in your network circle and how to connect with them. These strategies are essential when developing a healthy friendship that can lead to a future business relationship.

When you become an athlete, your goal is to win the championship. However, the overall picture requires you to look at the big picture, the teams you will compete against, and the individual players you will cover. The overarching goal is what comes to mind first and what you aspire to achieve. The strategies you need to put in place consist of the steps necessary to achieve the end result. Apply the same approach to your personal life as you change your mindset.

The paradigm shift in your personal life comes when you develop your long-term career goals. These goals should include maximizing your current opportunities and aligning them with your future goals and aspirations. Think about where you want to live, your future career path, and the money you need to accommodate your lifestyle. Use your time between seasons wisely, explore different careers, intern at a company, or shadow someone in the position you are interested in for a week or two. For example, Michael Thomas, New York Giants, worked for Representative Sheila Jackson Lee in DC as a part of the NFL leagues externship program. New Orleans Saints running back Alvin Kamara decided to get hands-on experience and sponsored a team at Daytona International Speedway. The best way to grow is to learn from people who are currently in the position you may one day want. I will delve deeper into this in the following chapters.

This may seem overwhelming at first when your mindset shifts from being an athlete to thinking about business deals and being an entrepreneur which can ultimately lead to mental barriers. A mental barrier is a self-limiting mindset and the most significant barrier. It is easy to experience a defensive failure, where you constantly think about something you want to do but do not take steps to move forward with that idea. If you decide to take action and make a mistake, this may prevent you from pursuing your goals. It may be easy to internalize your feelings without taking the first step. Or, you may think you are not good at it because you had a setback and do not enjoy your work. This leads to something we call the *imposter syndrome*. The imposter syndrome has you doubting all your thoughts, causing fear, and preventing you from moving forward. It becomes burdensome and unbearable. Because you internalized what you were thinking, you thought nothing worked, and you just want to give up. At this time it is vital to keep reminding yourself you are more than an athlete.

The saying "you are more than an athlete" requires you to expand and think deeply even when you do not want to. Let us try a different approach! It is not always comfortable stepping outside of your comfort zone. The unknown can be extremely frightening. One way to handle whatever you feel is by incorporating mindfulness into your daily routine and setting realistic goals. You are probably focused on the present and the current task at hand, which is playing. It may be hard, but each day you should say to yourself, "I am willing to try new things and get better at it," so during the off-season, explore as much as possible. Embrace the process that leads to the road to success and how you can apply and implement the strategies learned so far. Trust me. You have many transferable skills. It is just a matter of identifying the right talent and planning for your current situation. Let your imagination be your guide as you move forward.

Once you can visually see yourself doing whatever you want to do, it will shift how you see yourself. Self-talk will be instrumental in saying to yourself, "*I Can Do It*!" It is then you begin to understand that mistakes you made were lessons that helped you grow. Do not be afraid to make a mistake, or 50 mistakes for that matter. Mistakes are viewed as valuable information that can give you what you need to find a solution to a problem. For example: when you are playing, the coach calls a play, but you decide to do something different, which can be the difference between winning or losing the game. You fully understand the impact your decision can have, not only on you, but on the team as well. It is those types of situations that help you learn from your experience and how to make informed decisions based on the available information at hand. You can apply that same mindset to your personal life. Shifting from a fixed mindset may limit your belief that I am just good at being an athlete," to the growth mindset that tells you you can do whatever you want. Do not be afraid to follow the road less traveled or make a decision that is not favorable. You must keep plowing through.

Over time you learn not to avoid situations that appear to be challenging and how to embrace feedback. Rule of thumb: never compare yourself and what you are going through with others. This can lead to being subconsciously envious of others who appear to be making moves outside of playing. Your blueprint is designed for you; follow the path until the end. It is imperative to acknowledge your small progress or wins as an athlete and in your personal life because these are breakthroughs. Try to find momentum and incorporate positive thoughts to help you think more clearly and be proactive when solving problems. Start journaling what you are thinking about and how you feel while evolving. Replace those self-limiting beliefs with beliefs that empower you. Surround yourself with people who share the same interests. Make a mental note and visualize where you want to go.

It is vital to keep your environment calm and positive. Considering you work in a very competitive industry, this is one place you need a quiet place to just think. Declutter your mind and create space for new information continuously coming in. Because you are an athlete, people are constantly approaching you about something. I suggest only entertaining the people providing information that can add value to you and potentially be another income stream. Rule of thumb: never make a business decision without conducting research, asking a lot of questions, and resting your brain to process the information.

Before making any type of a decision, ensure you get the right amount of sleep, which is vital, so you do not go through mental exhaustion. Mental exhaustion can include not being organized and having unrealistic goals and expectations for others and yourself. Rethink how you spend your time and adjust your personal and work habits. This will be productive for optimal efficiency. Time is of the essence and often limited. Your time is already accounted for, so make the best use of your free time. During this time you are stretching, learning, and shifting from a fixed to a growth mindset.

The growth mindset allows you to keep progressing even when you encounter setbacks. Learning from mistakes and experiences helps you establish strategies such as eliminating overthinking, being embarrassed, worrying about what others think about you, and being a perfectionist. Manage your expectations. Get out, step outside of your comfort zone, and apply different strategies. As you go through this transitional phase, it is important to understand there are different stages you will go through as you leave one identity - being an athlete, for another - being the everyday person.

Trying to figure out what the future you will look like can be tiring and take time and effort. Everyone goes through it at one time or another in life. Williams Bridges, an organizational consultant, helps businesses and people going through these changes. Because he was vested in helping others, he created the *"Transitional Model"* to specifically identify the emotional stages and changes that occur during three stages while transitioning. In the first stage, he talks about *ending, losing, and letting go.* He defined emotions as fear, denial, anger, sadness, disorientation, a sense of loss, frustration, and uncertainty. In this stage, athletes find it really hard to accept the fact that playing and being an athlete is coming to an end. Resistance occurs during the change process when you do not accept or acknowledge these emotions. The transition process can only take place once playing altogether comes to an end.

Letting go is the most challenging part, but it allows you to enter this *neutral zone.* Imagine it is the end of your career, and you have no idea what to offer outside of sports. This in-between stage makes you feel like you are in limbo and not operating at the optimal level. Realigning your focus is critical during this stage. Shifting from the athlete's identity to a new identity requires you to learn and create new systems. Your emotions often go up and down, which can lead to confusion and distress. Once you accept what you are feeling, it becomes the foundation for your new beginning.

Your *new beginnings* require you to think differently, stretch, and grow out of your safe zone. In this new direction, you have a different understanding of your purpose and how you add value to any and everything you do. In addition, this new way of thinking gives you a sense of pride, confidence, and permission to move forward.

Remember, "every story has an end, but in life, every end is a new beginning." Relish every minute of being an athlete. You worked so hard to get to this *monumental moment* of becoming a professional athlete, but who said that has to be the last one? Life is like a book that consists of different chapters. You learn something new in each chapter you read, and you can apply it at some point. As you start to figure out your new identity, remember it is a gradual change, so be patient with yourself. It will not happen overnight.

LEVEL UP:

- How do you pivot from one career to another?
    - Start asking other athletes questions who have businesses and multiple streams of income coming in.
- What steps should you take to transition?
    - Pay attention to who is in your circle. Can they help you with other opportunities?
    - What businesses or organizations are close to where you play or your hometown can you develop partnerships with to work together?

- Be strategic about what you do and who you do it with. Do not jump on every boat that floats. You do not want to sink, if you are not prepared.
- Make the most out of your time during the season and the off-season. It would help if you had time to relax, spend time with your family, travel, and prepare for the next season. Allocate some time to work on a plan that consists of thinking about the future and your next steps.
- Take the same mindset that got you to the league and apply it as you prepare for your new identity.

CHAPTER THREE
Leverage and Monetize Your Current Platform and Brand

"If you don't give the market the story to talk about, they'll define your brand's story for you."
—David Brier.

Your brand is *YOU*. Your story. Your message. If you decide to write a book, you first learn that the title and cover are extremely important in capturing your audience's attention. You are the *book cover,* and the story you tell is your *brand message* or *brand story*. People are always watching, and your decisions can make or break you. Be very *clear* about your message. As Jeff Bezos once said, "Your brand is what other people say about you when you're not in the room." This is a profound statement. It is a constant reminder of the importance of being strategic and careful about the image you want the world to see and the story you share. It can be challenging being in that position, but the right connections can prepare you for your next job. There is power when you find your voice, so be consistent and use it wisely!

Be *consistent* and *intentional* with your brand messaging. When you show up regularly, it allows your audience to connect and engage with you entirely. "It" refers to companies or initiatives you align yourself with and the impact it has on your brand. Athletes who have endorsements with Brand Jordan go through a vetting process. Brand Jordan is very meticulous with its endorsements. The company looks at not only athletic abilities but also athlete's characteristic traits and the amount of community service done over the years. As a company, it is very important to ensure the people you bring to your team share the same values, philosophy, and vision. Seth Godin once said, "A brand is a set of expectations, memories, stories, and relationships that, taken together, account for the consumer's decision to choose one product or service over another." So be intentional with your brand messaging from the beginning.

As an athlete, it is critical to align yourself with companies that share your same vision and mission because of the long-term effect it can have on you. Your brand gives you access to a unique platform. Think about it. A brand influencer amplifies their brand through marketing on all social media platforms. They do so by being authentic when engaging with their targeted audience to create or promote content. Be *confident* about what you do and when you do it.

Your *confidence* will help you sell your service or product on all platforms. Whoever or whatever company you are affiliated with instantly correlates to your new identity once you are no longer an athlete. According to Richard Branson, "The brand that will thrive in the coming years are the ones that have a purpose beyond profit." So think about how your intentions and brand will impact others beyond the game.

If you are not active in the community outside of your work requirements, then I would argue that you are not capitalizing on all the opportunities you have as an athlete. Please make sure the causes or initiatives you are aligned with not only bring awareness to their product but to you too. Once you establish those partnerships, have a clear understanding of your role and how you are adding value to that company. Community partnerships open doors for additional tools and resources for whatever cause or initiative you are working on.

If we look at the climate in the world today, social and cultural change are at the top of the list and the main focus. The social impact athletes are making is transforming social beliefs and cultural norms that have existed for decades. Social impact means your vision and mission will ultimately be a blueprint for change. Currently, the world is focused on police reform and social inequalities, which was the beginning of a movement for change. It will not happen overnight, but with consistency, it will bring about new laws for how black and brown people are policed in communities. The only way to have a sustainable future is by understanding the process and having a system in place to support and reinforce that initiative. This is true not only for a business or social initiative but also for your personal brand.

Before the NBA, WNBA, and NFL resumed playing, there were stipulations and steps the players wanted to take place before the games began. During this time, athletes truly understood the immense impact and influence they had on what was happening around them. The decisions collectively started a movement, such as wearing the victims' names on uniforms or sneakers, standing in solidarity as a team for a cause and being the voice for the voiceless. In addition, platforms were leveraged, which started initiatives for companies to donate money to underserved communities and programs aligned with the cause. Remember to never underestimate your value and how to leverage your platform that will ultimately be used for the greater good.

As you create your brand, you need to start with your current platform and build upon it while playing. Elon Musk once said, "Brand is just a perception, and perception will match reality over time." It is not easy thinking about what your long-term brand will be. Considering rebranding requires you to shift your mindset and fully visualize the future. Therefore, it is critical to start the process immediately. During this manifestation process, you can use guided imagery to provide visualizations as a *blueprint* for how you proceed.

Manifestation requires you to be strategically innovative, specific about what you desire, and have a clear purpose and goals that will aid in the steps you take to define where you want to go. Your desires and goals will look different from the next person, but that is what makes you different. Give yourself permission to re-evaluate your identity and change it as needed. Trust the manifestation process as you pivot and uncover the lessons, gifts, or gems in every experience that will put you closer to what you define as success.

Remember, your brand is not only what you do but how you do it. Your brand should resonate with others; the only way to do that is to know your target audience. Then ask yourself this question: Do you share the same purpose as your audience, and if you need to connect with them, how do you connect with them? The goal is to define, organize, and position yourself where your brand is sustainable and prosperous. Leveraging your brand and platform is vital because you directly impact others in one way or another. Once you fully understand how to maximize your brand potential, you will stay ahead of the game. Your platform is *huge,* and if used correctly, it amplifies your voice. Utah Jazz's own Collin Sexton made his custom line of suitcases which is his signature brand. Considering he is following in the footsteps of Dwayne Wade, who has a partnership with Away luggage. To Sexton, it was a no-brainer considering you are always carrying a bag. Your role as an athlete is bigger than you, so do not take it for granted because it is a part of your legacy. It is essential to live in the present and prepare for the future *you* at the same time.

Bridging the gap between the old and new identity can be done simultaneously. Once you clearly define your purpose, it will provide you with a good foundation, guide you during your journey, and help with the decisions you make. This is where being creative and innovative will influence how you engage with others and do business. Having a mentor or coach to help you navigate is also essential; I will expand on that later. How you communicate and represent your brand will bring everything to life. Your identity tells your brand story in print, virtually, and physically. It should be seamless across all platforms. Your voice or messaging is powerful and is synonymous with your brand. Just think about what others will see. Tobias Harris, Philadelphia 76ers, is known for helping others in the community. He will have no problem fostering new relationships and partnerships because of the support he gives to others when he is not playing ball.

Here are a few quick tips on how to brand forward: your personal brand will evolve over time based on what is happening in the world and how you want others to see you. Be very specific and focused on the message you want to convey to each target audience demographic. Next, define your niche and stick to it. Finally, be consistent with your topic, which will be more memorable for people to relate to and remember, while others define you based on your niche topic.

Stay true to who you are by being authentic and genuine; it will go a long way. Your brand is more meaningful and purposeful. This will help your target audience be able to relate to you and who you are. Your reputation will succeed you no matter what. Humility is a personality trait that makes you likable and approachable. People always want to know your story and who you are on and off the court.

Tell your story and write your narrative as an athlete; people want to hear about your journey. Storytelling is an integral part of who you are. Your story should be engaging and with a flare of creativity. Understanding your platform and knowing how to implement brand marketing strategies will open up speaking engagements for you to connect with your audience. Start building your personal brand by sharing a story via a quick video on social media. Honestly, start a podcast and invite people on to interview. Video podcasting has grown among athletes. I like Draymond Green's unfiltered podcast because it allows players to share their feelings. This helps build confidence and speaking skills. During the pandemic, Clubhouse became a game-changer on many levels. The audience felt like they had a personal connection, which was super powerful. It is important to be in sync with your brand no matter what you do, where you are, and who you are with.

Be consistent with your appearance, content, and messaging across all platforms. Let us be clear - you will not always hit the mark with your target audience. You will sometimes take a hit and fail at connecting with them, but it is ok. Failure is a part of the process, and that is where resiliency comes into place. The best way to recover is to learn from your mistakes and start over again. Just think about it as if you had a bad game. How do you bounce back from that game? Do you go back out and play again? Same mindset, different challenges. The mental mindset allows you to push through and try something new, especially if you begin to doubt what you are doing and feel uncomfortable. Trial and errors are inevitable but do not dictate your future. Take the shot, hit the puck or ball, jump in the water, and run the field or track like no one is there but you. Don't let fear stop you from taking the first step.

Think about someone who inspires you and how their brand evolved over the years. Their journey and the many detours it took for them to get to where he or she is today probably was not easy. If you listen to their story, I am sure that person will share with you strategies he or she used to reach their platform. What advice do you think he/she would give you to do the same thing? Maybe something like following the market trends, doing your research before you jump in, and knowing the platforms to use and the culture for each social media platform is significant when learning how to communicate with your target audience. It reminds me of how your coach gives the plays to win and not lose the game. Your brand is similar to how you prepare and play the game. It's those memorable plays that people remember forever and constantly talk about. Make your brand work for you.

You are your brand all the time. The manifestation process has no time limit, so do not rush and jump headfirst. The initiatives you align yourself with should be a reflection of your values and beliefs. This will have a monumental impact on you as you grow.

Your legacy is a reflection of your personal brand. What are people saying about you on and off the court or field? People's perception of you is important because their conversations will help promote you to the next level. Let the people be a part of your PR and marketing plan. Word of mouth is the best marketing tool and strategy anyone can have at their disposal. It is free, and it travels fast.

For instance, if I say "Muhammad Ali," you would probably say he was the greatest boxer. But you also may say he was an advocate for social justice just like many players are today. Your reputation, name, and brand are all you have, so make sure it precedes you with everything positive. Over a lifetime, how do you want people to remember you? Your personal brand defines "Who you are" and your lasting impact on others. Make your legacy one people will never forget. When you begin the rebranding process, do it in small steps, not all at once. Embrace the process and have fun doing it.

Things that make you pause and reflect as you brand forward:

- Think about it, how have you used your platform?
- What is your brand message or brand story?
- Are you active in communities by volunteering your services?
- Do you have a foundation involved in the community where you play and or live?
- Do you have a partnership(s) with any company?

CHAPTER FOUR
Accept and Embrace the Process

"Every dream has a process and a price tag. Those who embrace the process and pay the price, live the dream. Those who don't, just dream."
—Jeremy Riddle.

Do not bury your dreams because of fear. You must take fear head-on. You have no choice but to accept and embrace the process because the process of change can be challenging. Be flexible and adapt to what is happening around you. "There are things we do not want to happen but have to accept, things we do not want to know but have to learn, and people we can't live without but have to let go." -Anonymous. During these times things can be very frustrating and challenging, even when you think you have it all together. Trying to figure out the steps you need to take can be overwhelming, to say the least. If all you had ever done was be an athlete, you might start to second guess your skill sets. That is when self-doubt comes in, and you start questioning your thought process and the decisions made thus far.

During this journey, you will have some barriers that will make you revisit who you are and where you are trying to go. This process can consist of feeling lost without the game, like something is missing, alone, or as if there is nowhere to turn. You do not want to be a part of the status quo who do not successfully pivot after the game. Do not get confused. This is a major shift in your life that can take 2 - 3 years to adjust to the new you. Considering you will be older and going through changes in your career, financially, physically, mentally, and friendships. The mere thought you will need to rebrand your identity will cause you to pause and re-evaluate your self-worth. You will also need to learn how to adapt to a new environment. This can be traumatic, depressing, and overwhelming.

The goal is for you not to become a prisoner of your own thoughts. In order to pivot successfully, ask for help because you are not alone. What you are experiencing and feeling is very normal. So, talk to other athletes who have gone through the process and use them as a support group, coach, or mentor. Failing forward is not an option. Developing an exit plan in advance would be essential and highly encouraged. I would also suggest seeing a counselor who can help you deal with any form of anxiety that may show up, and everything in your world appears to be amplified. A counselor can help if you suffer from any mental health issue and need a trained professional to provide interventions and strategies to implement during the transition. This level of support can give you the confidence needed to move forward, embrace the process, and prepare for the future.

The first step is to stay focused and establish a positive support system. Identify transferable skills such as being disciplined, being a team player, being able to perform under pressure, being goal-oriented, being a great leader, problem-solving, decision-making, and self-motivation. Envision what you can achieve by being prepared, and changing your mindset, attitudes, and behaviors while understanding the pitfalls during this process. Having positive images of oneself can help reduce anxiety about the future. Next, incorporate self-talk into your daily habits, including affirmations or meditation. Positive self-talk helps reduce negative emotions, makes you feel valued, stay motivated, and reminds you of all you set your mind to. Finally, you will need the self-control and concentration required for the next level.

Keep your goals at the forefront of your mind. You should make personal and professional goals and track them, if not daily, then weekly. As time passes, it is good to acquire information or feedback from your teammates, coaches, and friends about your skills and how they think they will resonate in your next career. This will provide critical information on what makes you different and stand out amongst everyone in your circle. Knowing how people see you is vital to how you see yourself. This will allow time for you to work on self-improvement and realigning everything in your life.

The process will make you aware of what is happening around you. It will also teach you how to adjust to situations as they arise and make decisions based on the available information. The information you acquire will be vital and helpful as you prepare for your next chapter. Learn to ask questions from people who will provide feedback to help you evolve into the next version of yourself. Stay focused. Apply what you learned from your experiences as an athlete, and do not be afraid to ask for help if needed. There is no time to have a lot of pride on this journey. Remember, changing the mindset is the only way to stretch and grow. It may be during this time you start to think about generating different sources of income that add value to others and make an impact. Have you considered how to maximize your 501c3 and make it work for you? Your foundation can be a viable business if aligned with the right causes or businesses.

If you have a foundation, it can be another source of income and a great business to grow while making a social impact in communities.

CHAPTER FIVE

Your Foundation Presence in Communities

"True wealth is not measured in money or status or power. It is measured in the legacy we leave behind for those we love and those we inspire."
—Cesar Chavez.

Your legacy and impact will be defined by the value you add to others and communities. Illuminate your platform by cultivating positive partnerships with schools by implementing and managing your signature brand education or sports programs in schools. You could also open your own charter school, daycares - learning centers, shelters for people in transition, or group homes for children, to name a few.

Having a nonprofit organization is one of the best-kept secrets out there. Athletes are encouraged to have a foundation, especially for the financial benefits that come along with it. As a business, it can be viable in communities. The only way to optimize your foundation is to operate it as a Fortune 500 company. Remember, this can ultimately be another stream of income while you are playing, and when ready to pivot for life beyond the game, your foundation can be functional, sustainable, and operational.

Growing and sustaining your business requires you to have the right board members on your team and a good infrastructure. As a consultant, I often see the common trends and mistakes made by not having the right people on the board. Usually, the initial thought most athletes have is this is something their parents, guardians, siblings, family, or friends can run. That is all fine and good; however, the problem arises, like anything else, if you are not prepared to take on such a massive undertaking, it can be exhausting and mentally overwhelming.

If this is the case, provide your team with the right tools to be intentional and effective in their decisions. The goal and objective should not be for the foundation to stay afloat while you are playing. But to make a social impact, grow the business, provide jobs not only for family and friends but people in the community, and, last but not least, generate additional revenue while you are playing and for retirement.

It is essential to have members who share the same vision, mission, and values. I have said this many times, but honestly, I cannot stress it enough. You do not need anyone on your team with a hidden agenda because it will eventually come to light. Your board members should have diverse skill sets and access to additional resources. It is critical to ensure your members are well-versed in the area they will oversee. If they need to gain experience or expertise in an area, provide them with the necessary tools needed so they can be effective when it comes to making informed decisions. Your vetting process should include an intensive and extensive background review of the people you are considering for your board. Your board should consist of an accountant, a lawyer, an educator, a publicist/marketing specialist, a parent, a social worker, a community leader, a realtor, and other professional backgrounds depending on the overall goal of your foundation.

For example, if one of your parents or family members takes on the role and responsibility of being the president or vice president, be certain they know and understand their job description. The responsibilities can include but are not limited to, ensuring the vision and mission of the foundation maintains its core values, goals, and objectives. In addition, the president or vice president will develop and implement strategic short and long-term plans, policies, and procedures, manage all employees, oversee daily operations, create job descriptions, and manage the hiring of employees/volunteers. The overarching objective is to ensure all goals are achieved in a realistic timeframe, the foundation is visible in targeted communities, and there is effective and fluent communication between the founder and the board members.

I listed the responsibilities because this is a full-time job. It is vital to thoroughly think through the qualifications your board will need, and the recruiting and onboarding processing. The organization's infrastructure has to be structured for continual growth and sustainability. I strongly suggest you have a *S.W.O.T.* analysis conducted which is a strategic planning technique that identifies the foundation *Strengths*, *Weaknesses*, *Opportunities*, and *Threats* related to the long-term planning process. And then, do a *GAP* and *Market* analysis that will help identify market trends and how to bridge any gaps in that industry.

Athletes running their camps during the offseason allows youth from those communities to interact and engage in structured activities while interacting with professional athletes and entertainers they would never come in contact with. Think about the amount of money spent on hosting a camp, how much money is out of pocket expense and or from a sponsor? Do you usually break even or raise a small amount of money for the nonprofit organization you partner with, such as the Boys and Girls Club, youth program, shelter, hospital, or school?

I know many athletes use the foundation for tax write-offs, which is fine. However, your foundation is a business that can employ people from the community. It can provide additional resources to those who need help finding a job. This can be a great way to create generational wealth and a legacy while serving others. Having a return on your investment is essential, but what is even more important is the impact you will have overall in those communities you serve.

Here is a quick tip: for those of you who have been looking for opportunities in education, your foundation is what you need to enter the education sector, which includes providing instruction and training in K-12 schools, afterschool centers, or tutoring. I know many athletes trying to figure out how to open a charter school, like Lebron James, Jalen Rose, or Kevin Durant's afterschool center. Russell and Ciara Wilson have recently invested funds to rebrand a charter school in Seattle that was having challenges staying open. You do not always have to start from the beginning. You can invest and become a part of the process and turn around a school providing students in underserved communities with opportunities they never had. There are so many options. For example, Aaron Gordon, who plays for the Denver Nuggets, foundation has a partnership with the University of Central Florida to launch a STEM program for underserved children during the summer months from 2021 - 2025.

Education is not something you can figure out as you go, but it is possible to do with the right people on your team, such as my company. Therefore, it is advantageous for you to find the right partnerships to provide additional resources and jobs and meet your desire to make a social impact while bringing awareness to a cause you are passionate about and supporting others.

Here are a few essential questions you should be able to answer with ease:

- When you think about your foundation, is it adding value to communities?
- Have you cultivated meaningful partnerships to further your foundation's vision and mission?
- Is your foundation's infrastructure set up for long-term sustainability or profitability?

On the other hand, if pursuing an opportunity in education is not for you, and you want to explore different professions, you still can apply these same practical steps and strategies as you try to figure out what the business version of you looks like.

CHAPTER SIX

Career Development and the Business

Version of You
*"Setting goals is the first step in turning
the invisible into the visible."*
—Tony Robbins

What does the business version of you look like? The quest to find a new career can be exciting and rewarding. However, this is the part of the journey where you must be in tune with who you are. Identify your passions, skills, and what you bring to the table. Career development is the preparation you will need as you shift your mindset from being an athlete to a professional. This lifelong process consists of various factors to ensure you are on the right track.

If you look at it from this perspective, you already have your first job that provides you with a lot of on-the-job training and support. Take advantage of all the resources you have as a player and work on developing your post-career plan. The decisions you make for your future career impact you and your family, including the lifestyle you have grown accustomed to. Malcolm X once said, "The future belongs to those who prepare for it today." Developing a career plan will be one of the most important steps you make when preparing for your next move.

Benjamin Franklin once said, "By failing to prepare, you are preparing to fail." Career planning is not just for the moment; it is a plan that will continually evolve as you evolve. This will require you to self-reflect and identify your interests, skills, values, and abilities. Then, start evaluating your career options and explore opportunities. Once you start writing down your career goals, use it as a *roadmap* to provide you with directions on how to get from Point A to Point B. This map will help you make the best decisions and expand your knowledge, improving your skills and broadening your overall goals.

Career development and planning will not occur overnight; it is definitely a process. Think of it as planning and managing your future career all at one time. Confucius said, "Success depends upon previous preparation, and without such preparation, there is sure to be a failure." So take small steps and strides at your own pace. Do not stress yourself out because you possess many of the traits employers are looking for, which are equivalent to your strengths.

As an athlete, you have already shown your future employer who you are and what you bring to the table. Those strengths are being goal-oriented, performing well under pressure, being ambitious, analytical, data-driven, making sound decisions, and developing and effectively executing a plan. The goal is to communicate your achievements and wins with no problem.

Here are a few practical strategies you can apply: **be flexible** and not be so hard on yourself. This is a work in progress. Be *accountable* for your behaviors and attitudes. This is about you, and it is your journey. No one can tell you how you should feel, but let others guide you in the process.

You are a **lifelong learner**, so it will be imperative to research your areas of interest and understand what skills you need to reach your goals. Then *invest* in yourself by continuing your education or exploring business opportunities, such as investments or partnerships.

Challenge yourself to step out of your comfort zone. This is where you do things differently, but you must be willing to take the risk and jump.

Get *help*. Do not be afraid to say, "I am struggling and I do not know where to start or what to do." You will not be the first or last person to feel clueless. This is the perfect time to have a great support system in place.

Affirmations should be a daily part of your routine. You are who you say you are, so continue to replace those negative thoughts with positive thoughts, affirming your beliefs.

This is a time of resiliency, especially when those negative thoughts start to creep into your mind. A strong internal drive is needed to prepare for your next chapter. This identity change will be drastic, so putting practices in place will help you once that change begins.

Do not be afraid to ask questions because, as you know, a closed mouth doesn't get fed. However, now is not the time to be quiet. Thinking deeply requires you to delve deep and really think about your future career aspirations. Remember, acquiring your dream job does require some form of preparation. An author once said, "Success is when persistence meets preparation." This is what is needed to make this somewhat of a seamless transition.

As you develop your career plan and the paths you would like to explore, start researching those jobs on sites such as Indeed, Glassdoor, or LinkedIn, to name a few. The goal is to look at the descriptions and the requirements. This information will be good to know because it will provide you with a baseline of your skills and qualifications. Then, you can revisit your plan and add the steps necessary to meet those additional job description requirements. Looking at these job descriptions will also help you identify the trends in keywords that are being used during that time. Start writing down and keep track of those words because you can use them on your resume.

Here is a quick tip many people need to think about doing: join Toastmasters. In case you are unfamiliar with Toastmasters, it is an international public speaking club that consists of a group of people from different professional backgrounds who come together two times a month to work on their leadership and communication skills.

Toastmasters' goals are to help individuals improve their self-confidence and personal growth by having the ability to communicate with others effectively. It increases your confidence when preparing for a job interview or presentation. Toastmasters sharpen skills such as leadership, listening, planning, motivating others, and team building. This is a great way to expand your networking community and obtain support while honing in on those skills. You never know. You could be potentially sitting next to your future boss or business partner.

The story's moral is that you do not have to feel like you are on an island by yourself. You can invest in a career development coach if you need assistance and guidance. A career coach can help you create a career plan, identify those transferable skills, write your resume, role-play interviews, make realistic goals, and determine if you need to go back to school or if you have the skills for the job you are seeking. They can also help you explore options such as working for someone else, growing your foundation, or being an entrepreneur.

Here is some food for thought:

- What will the next version of you actually look like?
- Have you fully capitalized on various opportunities that came your way to try new things? Such as internships or shadowing someone for a day?
- Do you have a resume? If not, do you need help with writing one?
- Do you need to refresh those interviewing skills?
- Do you need to go back to school or plan to return to school to finish your education?
- What resources do you need to help you prepare for your future?

Knowing and understanding what you need will be valuable information to take the necessary steps to move forward. During this phase, Vernon Howard said, "Run forward when possible, walk ahead when you can, stagger onward when you must, but never cease your forward movement." No matter what you do, always continue working on your plan.

While you are currently playing, think about those creative skills you have and how you can turn that into a business. Of course, being an entrepreneur has advantages, so let us figure out what those entrepreneurial skills are.

CHAPTER SEVEN
Entrepreneurship

"Don't worry about being successful but work toward being significant and the success will naturally follow."
—Oprah Winfrey

Have you heard that old saying, "Don't wait for opportunity. *Create it.*" If you do not want to work for anyone, then being an entrepreneur may be the direction you want to follow. You are probably an entrepreneur at heart.

Honestly, being an athlete, you are already demonstrating those entrepreneurial and leadership skills. For example, you understand the importance of having the right people on your team. Over the years, you had to trust the information given to you and align your decisions with your passion, purpose, and aspirations. As an entrepreneur, you are the *CEO*, Chief Executive Officer, of your powerhouse, which is *YOU*. The people on your team work for you, such as your agent, management team, financial planner, and anyone else you employ.

As the *CEO*, let us take a deep dive into your business and how to monetize those skills. Before and after games and practices, you have the opportunity to speak to reporters. Every time you are interviewed, you are working on your communication skills and learning to listen to questions and effectively articulate your response. Those questions can be edited and reformatted to meet your needs for your podcast, syndicated television or radio show, or online magazine. No need to reinvent the wheel - tweak it to fit your needs.

What if you still need to capture who you are fully? That is where the importance of identifying things you are passionate about is valuable. You have so many resources, and now more than ever is the time to tap into them. The one piece of advice I will strongly suggest is if you decide to start your own business, make sure you have someone on your team who knows how to set up a business and the company's infrastructure.

The infrastructure is the company's blueprint. The blueprint includes the vision, mission, philosophy, strategic plan, job descriptions, onboarding, and salary, to name a few. While your company infrastructure is being developed, it is critical to conduct a *SWOT* analysis for *Strengths, Weaknesses, Opportunities, and Threats*. I mentioned the SWOT analysis in the previous chapter. In case you forgot, the SWOT analysis ensures your company is running at an optimal level and has what it needs - the right plan and resources - to be successful. These are the nuts and bolts of your company's daily operation and function. I know many people will tell you to jump first, but those who jump without a plan are the ones whose companies are not sustainable and are out of business within one to five years. An African Proverb says, "For tomorrow belongs to people who prepare for it today."

Being an entrepreneur is knowing how to navigate and make informed and effective decisions based on the readily available information you have. Do your research and take the time to understand your business industry. Do not have *yes* people on your team who are afraid to give you the right information because they do not want to go against the grain. The wrong information will have you looking uninformed and unprepared. Do not have people on your team who do not share information because then it positions you as being clueless and out of the loop about your own business. Instead, have people around you who are more knowledgeable and help you achieve your goals.

Stay Woke! Rome was not built in a day or overnight. This is a process and the long-term goal is to ensure successfully grow and sustain your business. Steph Curry once said, "Success is not an accident. Success is actually a choice." Success will look different for everyone, so do not let others define it for you.

This is definitely one concept athletes struggle with: which is once you stop playing, you will no longer be in the public eye as much, if not any, which will make it harder to find support and often opportunities. So everything you do has to be intentional while you are playing. "To be successful, you must be intentional." When you look at the future through those lenses, you will begin to understand the sense of urgency. The goal is for you to try new things and not reinvent the wheel if you do not have to. But if you want to reinvent the wheel, make sure you have the right people around you when you do.

Like many, athletes often make the same mistakes, wanting to help everybody and thinking everyone has their best interest at heart. This is one of the hardest lessons because athletes often need to take a step back and thoroughly vet people before doing business with them. Just remember, before you say I do; be honest with yourself and think about the background check and homework you do before moving forward to ensure the person you are dealing with is trustworthy and credible in their expertise. Preparedness is essential, so covering all angles will be vital for the next phase when exploring new opportunities. At this point, it is important to define what success looks like for you as you establish your short and long-term goals.

While playing, learn how to leverage and monetize your current platform by strategically marketing everything you do. For example, know the influencers and key players in the industry your company affiliate with moving forward. Show up to events with the intention and sole purpose of networking.

I will use my former client Bobby Taylor (B.T.), who played for the Philadelphia Eagles, as an example. As his publicist and brand marketing strategist, my job was to make him visible in the public's eye. I developed a strategic marketing plan that focused on his desires and passions. For example, Bobby wanted to model and have a television and a radio show. My goal was to leverage and monetize his brand and business simultaneously.

My plan consisted of making sure he was on every VIP guest list in New York, where he could network and be in the presence of the people he wanted to converse with and possibly lead to a business opportunity. I never forget attending an industry event with the executives from this business who wanted to hire B.T.. We sat at the VIP table with the executives and now CBS Morning Show host Gayle King. It was such a memorable moment, but also a viable connection. After that event, the sunglasses company that sponsored the event hired Bobby as one of their models. From there, I got Bobby a deal with Comcast, where he had his own Monday night pregame football television show. He also co-hosted a Monday Night football radio show with Wendy Williams and Colby Colb at Power 99 FM. This is how you leverage and monetize with purpose.

However, there are other players we can look at who have been making moves in the industry. For example, Lebron James has not only made his guest appearances on screen, but he is an executive producer and owns his own production company, Springhill Entertainment, and media brand, Uninterrupted. In addition, he has 19 Blaze Pizza franchises and has minority ownership in an English Soccer team in Liverpool.

Charles Woodson is a Wine Purveyor and partners with a well-known winemaker; and is in the process of launching his own wine, Twentyfour. Alex Rodriguez is the franchise owner of several UFC Gyms. Dwyane Wade invested in BallerTV, which streams live youth sports. Now anyone can watch this amazing young talent when they play. This is major and a game-changer. During the season and off-season, maximize your time wisely and efficiently by exploring untapped skills and potential connections.

Just do me one favor as an entrepreneur: remember this as you begin this amazing journey, "Your value doesn't decrease based on someone's inability to see your worth." ~Anonymous. Every move you make, make it with the *intent* to *WIN*! Do not let anyone define who you are. Instead, you define yourself and make sure they see you from your point of view and not theirs.

CHAPTER EIGHT
Know Your Worth

*"Success is not about how much money you make.
It's about the difference you make in people's lives."*
—Michelle Obama

You have this monumental platform and endless resources and often do not fully capitalize from it. When you are drafted, you are still very young and growing, so planning ahead is far from the first thing you think about. However, you have the world in your hands. And this type of notoriety is a lot to acquire at once.

No crash course that fully explains how one should feel or what one should do, especially when you become an athlete, considering everyone comes from different backgrounds. Some of you may have a sense of urgency to establish stability for your family. For others, it could be the opportunity to be independent and fulfill your dream of being a part of a professional team. Either way, without the proper guidance and support, your time playing will go by fast, and a large percentage of athletes will not be financially prepared to leave the game when it is time.

I say this because I want you to make good decisions. There are so many people out there who will promise you the world if you go into business with them. They know your worth, what you bring to the table, and how to use you to their advantage. If they know your worth, you to know your worth. So before you entertain that conversation, "know your worth, then add tax."-Anonymous

Face it you may not be the star player on the team, but you are a part of a professional team that carries a lot of weight. "Make sure you don't start seeing yourself through the eyes of those who don't value you. Know your worth, even if they don't." Sometimes, you may come across people who take you for granted and make you feel like you need them. You need to watch those people because they may have a hidden agenda. Be careful about the company you keep.

Times have changed immensely over the years. I see more athletes reading about potential investments, paying attention to the business world, and asking the right people the right questions. Research is such a viable tool anyone can use. Numbers never lie; the data you acquire will help you understand the market you are trying to get into and how to effectively and strategically capitalize from it.

More people are starting to pay attention to analytics. Data collection is used all the time to determine many things. For example, let us look at social media and your number of followers. The daily or weekly analytics tell you the best day and hour to post. It also provides you with demographic information, so you know specifically who your target audience is. The goal is to take that information and monetize it.

During the pandemic, Esports were at an all-time high. It was exciting to watch athletes play live or, at times, join a random game to have fun. Data were collected from surveys, polls, and analytics to determine what games to televise or go live on social media and the days and times people tuned in to watch. That information and algorithm determined how much money a player was paid based on the results. Companies use this information to determine the most effective and efficient marketing and advertising methods. This information was also used to decide whose face(s) should grace the cover for digital advertising and marketing promotions.

You can take that same approach when understanding your value in the market. A quick poll or survey will give you the information you need to know when you are trying to figure out how valuable you are, or will be, in the business world. Do not undervalue yourself because you did not do your homework. Trust me. The company you are affiliated with researched everything about you, and they understand your value and worth. There are culminating factors they consider before considering doing business with you.

This goes both ways. When you are hosting an event and looking for sponsors, companies and people become sponsors because they want to be associated with you. Depending on how the event is marketed and where their banners are placed during the event is very important. This is factored in when deciding what package they will take. The media coverage that comes with it is extremely valuable, and that company or person understands how it will increase their sales over the long run. In addition, the ongoing advertisement the company will do, from the number of pictures or videos taken and posted, will drive business their way.

Do not let self-limiting thoughts prevent you from asking anybody what they think your worth is. Think about your agent. Their job is to ensure you have the best contract based on what you can do for the team, your potential to help the team meet their goals, and the overall value you add, especially in areas where they might be weak. Your agent will always work in your best interest because they know your worth.

Another example is endorsements. You are a walking billboard for that product. Think about how many people buy that brand because of you. You may not have all the information at first, but the next time you renegotiate, ask for that data monetization. This will help you determine how valuable you are to that company. Now you have what you need to negotiate effectively.

The story's moral is not to underestimate what you bring to the table. Do not overthink it because that is where you get stuck. Then it becomes a spiraling effect due to fear and doubt you begin to have. You know what you can produce; you need the right opportunity and support team to help you reach your full potential. Doing your homework is essential. Stay focused and consistent. Be prepared and committed to making it work, even if you step outside your comfort zone. Embrace the process as you move forward.

Before you sit down for a business meeting, know your worth and accept nothing less. If you are unsure about how to make this decision on your own, you should have a coach or mentor who can help answer those questions. Someone who has been in your shoes, understands what you are going through, and can advise you on how to move forward even while playing.

CHAPTER NINE
The Value of Having a Mentor

"Someone who allows you to see the hope inside yourself."
—Oprah Winfrey

Having a mentor in your life will be a game-changer on many levels. A mentor comes with extensive knowledge, resources, and tools you will need in your career of interest. He or she can help you navigate a complex and ever-changing world. Finally, the ability to form meaningful connections in their vast and diverse network will be extremely valuable.

Let me be clear. You want a mentor who will add value; if your mentor does not, it is time to get a new one. Mentors will aid in building your confidence level in areas where you may struggle and help you think outside the box. You can have more than one mentor. Each person brings different perspectives and solutions to the table when needed. I am not saying you need a lot of mentors, but one will be beneficial, especially if you are entering unknown territory.

A mentor should help you fulfill your goals and bring your vision to life. The goal is to help you improve everything you do and want to do. When you have that person around, your energy and vibrational frequency are very high. They help you reach a new level, not steal the spotlight from you. You know the areas where you are weak. That person should be able to help you strengthen those areas, help expand your vision, and generate *wins* along the way. You can only generate wins if you are equipped with the right tools and resources.

You play an intricate part in the type of people you attract to be on your team. Do you exhibit a leadership attitude? Meaning, "I can do whatever I set my mind to." Do you like being in control and successful in whatever you do? Your circle should consist of the same type of people who share that same mindset. This is how you continue to grow, and honestly, you are helping your team grow and stretch because your expectations are high. The synergy should elicit creativity and ideas on how to reach your full potential.

However, if you decide to explore being an entrepreneur, having a mentor can definitely help guide and provide you with a wealth of knowledge. A good mentor will never tell you what you want to hear to make you feel good. He or she will be honest with you. The goal is not to make you feel bad but to help identify your strengths and weaknesses. This information helps with developing practical strategies for improvement in those areas. To grow, you cannot have an ego, and really there is no time for one. The focus is to stimulate your personal and professional goals, allowing you to reimagine who you are or want to be. You do want to be confident - just not arrogant.

A mentor will not take credit for your accomplishments. He or she will encourage and empower you to keep going even when you want to stop. They often create boundaries and priorities that keep you organized and focused on the overarching goals. This is your journey; they guide you to achieve success.

Think about the people you have crossed paths with, and you experience synergy with that person. As an athlete, is there someone on your team who is always positive and makes moves? Someone who encourages others to try new things and follow their dreams? What about the NBPA, WNBPA, NFLPA, MLSPA, NHLPA, MLSPA, Nascar, or Golf, for example? There is someone at one of these associations who can provide you insight on how to navigate as an athlete, share their story about some of the mistakes they experienced, and advice on how not to repeat the same mistakes. He or she will be pivotal in helping you because they already know what and how you are feeling.

Even when you have a thousand and one ideas, a good mentor will listen and provide feedback on whether you should follow your instincts or walk away. Candor is something you may have to get used to. But you will want him or her to be genuine and authentic no matter what. It is not personal. It is about what is in your best interest. Your mentor may even have connections in place for you to move forward.

Last but not least, mentors want you to win to be successful. Therefore, mentors are vested in you and will add value no matter what you do. Such an example is Lebron who has been mentoring Quinn Cook teaching him how to leverage and monetize his platform. As a result, Quinn wrote a children's book and partnered with Recruiting Platform STAC to provide resources for student-athletes. Do not take a mentor's presence for granted; learn everything you can and apply as needed. Having a mentor shows you are ready to make the right choice because they will help you be well-versed and equipped with what you need to succeed.

Think of an idea(s) you have or had in the past. Is it a dream deferred, or did you act on trying to bring it to life? Think about if you had a vision and left it as a dream with no action. Think about why you should have taken the steps needed to move forward. Is it because you needed the right people on your team to bounce ideas off? Did the people on your team understand the vision but needed to learn how to help you bring your vision to fruition? If this happened, did you reach out to someone who could help you? The flip side is, did you try to accomplish your goals but become discouraged because you needed to have all the information and resources needed to move forward so you just gave up? If so, did you realize you needed someone on your team who could help you take your vision, breathe fresh air into it, and bring it to life? That is what a good mentor can do for you.

The way you view opportunities is significant. Keep a positive attitude. Your positivity will help others stay positive and is an excellent indicator of future success. This is where the vibrational frequency is at its highest, and the people around you feed off you. They should inspire you to keep pushing when your energy level is down because that is the type of environment you want to be created amongst your team.

Do not bring negative people on this part of your journey. They will never understand what you are doing even if you explain it to them one hundred times. It is okay; it's just a reality check. They should not and cannot be on this part of the journey with you. You do not want to have anyone draining all your energy and ultimately sowing doubt, even if that is not their intention. It is simple; they cannot see your vision because it is not theirs. It would help if you had cheerleaders on your team who would keep motivating you even when you get tired.

Always remember you can have more than one mentor. But whoever you bring on your team should understand the direction you are going in and can help you along the way. Think of the people around you right now who you trust, and have a good relationship with, and are successful in your eyes. Even if you do not know that person well, it will not hurt to reach out to them to ask for help. Whoever it is, make sure he/she is committed to helping you get to the next level. You both need to share that same type of commitment to obtain the level of success you are trying to achieve.

For example, when trying to get to the league, you are committed to the process and will do whatever it takes to make it happen. You need the right coach to provide you with plays and opportunities to show what you are capable of. It would help if you have a good strength and conditioning coach, nutritionist, etc... you get the point. Each level you make it to requires different strategies and teams. Everyone on your team is committed to seeing you win and be successful. It is inevitable to keep you from success when you have a good mentor who believes in you. The goal is to keep you moving forward no matter how difficult it becomes. Those barriers you face should eventually become stepping stones because you learned how to use them to your advantage and did not allow them to defeat you.

Quick recap: when you are looking for a mentor(s) or people to be on your team, they should share similar ideas and have a vision of how to help you be successful. You and no one else defines success. Listed below are essential character traits your mentor should have:

1. Authentic/ Transparent
2. Honest
3. Loyal and committed to your vision and mission
4. Good listener
5. Knowledgeable and Resourceful
6. Provide constructive feedback
7. Non-Judgemental
8. Flexible and bringing a different perspective
9. Understand the power of networking
10. Successful in their career

Now is the time to think about who is on your team and how they can help you reach your full potential and success beyond your dreams. Are they setting you up for success?

CHAPTER TEN
The Art of Networking

"Understand that networking is an ongoing process, not a discrete event. Success comes from consistently making new contacts, following up, and keeping in touch."
—Anonymous

The art of networking is a skill one develops over time. It is consistent communication with someone while developing a positive relationship. It is one of the most powerful tools you should readily have available. An established network allows you to expand and build relationships personally and professionally. You can easily gain insight into a career you are interested in and provide access to opportunities, executives, or owners of businesses you would not usually have.

According to Bill Gates, "Power comes not from knowledge kept but from knowledge shared." Networking is knowledge shared and advice provided on how to effectively navigate when trying to learn or improve your skill set. This is an ongoing process of connecting with others who can potentially help you. Having the right people around you is essential, especially ones with whom you can bounce ideas off and who can give you good advice.

The next time you attend an event, make sure you walk away with at least three new contacts. The next day, send a quick text or email saying it was a pleasure meeting them, where you met, and that you look forward to connecting with them soon. The following week send a quick text or email based on their preferred method of communication and schedule a time to meet with them within the next week or two. Remember to send a quick thank you. The CEO of AJax said, "Behind every successful person, there are many successful relationships." If you look at it from a different point of view, networking is a form of generating money. Grow your network, and do not put a limit on your net worth.

Be strategic when networking, so you feel confident because you have yet to get your desired response immediately. People and the company's marketing teams pay attention to everything you do. Even when you are playing, they look at how many fans scream your name during the game. Why is that important? It shows you have a fan base and how they can generate money if you are a part of their company's team. Do you know how many of your jerseys are being sold during the season versus the off-season? Stores use this data to determine where your jersey will be placed in stores. And how many of them should they keep in stock during those times? Who is making that decision at that store, and how can you meet them? Is it beneficial to contact those people, or that person, and see if they would be interested in selling your products? Trust me; they may be more excited to meet with you than you are with them.

People who value your work, on and off the court or field, will always work with you. Your job is to know who these people are. Be intentional, authentic, and transparent when you network. Some people are charismatic and can attract the people they want to do business with. However, that will only take you so far. You must be prepared to close the deal. If you wing it, they will know because you cannot answer their questions. Not only is that embarrassing, but you may not get that opportunity again.

Do you remember when you first learned a scout was coming to the game to watch you play? The preparation and research you did to prepare for that interview were extensive. Someone might have told you the types of questions they would ask, but not all the questions. I am sure you have been told before they make a final decision if you would be the right fit for their team. They do a background check on how you interact with others and the type of people you surround yourself with. They may not have to go far because social media gives them an insight into who you are. If you do your homework right, you will have a good sense of the schools that scouts usually visit. Networking with the right people may fill in those blanks along the way.

Stay focused on your goals and what you are trying to achieve. Having the right people on your team can help with networking and meeting the people who can take you to the next level. This should not feel or look like a transaction at a store, but the first step to cultivating a relationship with someone who has the power and means to connect the dots for you. The initial meeting is like the first interview, so understand how valuable the opportunity is and ask questions if you need the best approach to use. This is a time to use your active listening skills because that person will provide you with a lot of information. Do not stop there. Be strategic, empathetic, and consistent to make it to the second interview, where the question will be asked why they should invest in you.

Networking is a form of storytelling that aims to elicit emotions. If you do your homework right, you can tell the story from a different perspective. You can talk about the pain points you've identified at their company and how you are the right and only person who can help provide a solution. Your pitch needs to be concise and to the point. Practice your pitch often. Use your phone to record yourself making the pitch. This will help you immensely. Once you hear what the other person hears, you can modify it as often as you want until you get it right. Practice... Practice... Practice! Practice makes perfect.

You are not a salesperson but trying to sell your services. You have 2-3 minutes to nail your pitch. Strike up a conversation and feel the person out. Talk about the things you are passionate about. That person may share the same passion. Ask them questions, listen, and find out their interests while building a rapport. Meet them where they are by approaching them on their level. Identify your strengths and articulate and illuminate the value you will bring to the table. Your body language is constantly talking, so be mindful of that. Be aware of your facial expressions. Your handshake should be firm. Speak with confidence. Your approach speaks volumes. Try to develop a system that works best for you regarding networking. If it is a system, you can constantly rehearse your moves until it becomes natural. Some people are natural networkers, and that is ok. It is like being an athlete; you practice the plays you like and add them to the game when you get the opportunity.

I cannot stress this enough... be intentional and strategic when networking. Please do not make it all about you even though you understand it may be all about you. Authenticity and transparency go a long way. Remember the desired outcome you are trying to accomplish by meeting that person. How can you convey your message where it resonates, and the other person is eager to further the conversation?

Once that person buys in, you must be committed to the process. It is an excellent opportunity to expand your network and reach your goals much faster. You will continue to grow if you follow the 3 P's (*Plan, Prepare, and Practice*).

CHAPTER ELEVEN
Plan Forward

"A goal without a plan is a wish."
—Author Unknown

Starting over can be daunting because it requires you to be flexible even as you plan for life beyond the game. Therefore, it is imperative to start preparing for the future while you are currently playing. Preparation is key and a process, so be patient with yourself. Continue to try as many different things as possible because, during this time, you can figure out what you like and do not like to do.

Self-awareness is essential and helps you be in tune with what is happening in different environments. This time can be stressful and traumatic because it is unfamiliar territory, but staying committed requires you to think at a different level. Think of this time as trial and error, so if you mess up, you can start over or move on to the next challenge. The best way to deal with emotional trauma is to start by setting goals.

Goal setting allows you to step out of your safe zone and embrace what you do not know and the pain you will endure when you encounter adversity. Staying humble and selfless allows you to build a great networking system that could eventually be your greatest ally when it is time to transition. Identify short and long-term goals and work towards them. Remain disciplined as your attitude and behaviors change. Always remember the next version of you requires a different version of you. You cannot stay the same and expect a different outcome. "If the plan doesn't work, change the plan, not the goal." The great thing about setting goals is you can change them based on where you are in your life.

Setting *SMART* goals, goals that are *specific, measurable, achievable, realistic, and timely*, would be beneficial and practical. Those practical goals remind you that you can accomplish anything you set your mind to. When goals are visible, they are more attainable, so use tactical tools to execute your plan and meet your objectives. If you can visualize your goal, you can achieve it.

You have to believe you can reach those goals and do whatever you say you can do. Always remind yourself not to have strict and rigid expectations because that might become burdensome. Self-reflection and self-awareness allow you to reexamine and revise your goals as needed, so if you do not accomplish them, you modify your goal.

Be aware of and acknowledge your current achievements, whether small or big. The ability to make progress is always a win that can turn into multiple wins. Good life skills, such as effectively communicating with others, being humble, leading, conflict resolution, and persevering through challenging times, are critical for self-improvement and performance skills, both on and off the court.

Your goals should align with the vision of what your new identity will look like in the future. Your attitude and beliefs should be positive when you approach any situation. When encountering setbacks or unfortunate circumstances, pivot and focus on something positive, do not let your bad experiences dictate your future goals or success. Self-motivation is essential at all times.

Eventually, when you retire, there will be drastic changes in your life, such as your routines and responsibilities, no longer being a part of the team, and not having someone to talk to as needed, like your coach or teammates. Pay attention to the people around you, such as your teammates, coaches, or front office staff, and try cultivating friendships with those you can trust. Then, start planning and moving forward. Fichtner said, "Planning without action; is futile, action without planning is fatal."

Keep in the front of your mind what I said before - the next version of you requires a different version of you. Let nothing and no one prevent you from embracing the shift in your identity. Be *proud, confident, and courageous* as the rebranding begins. You are more than an athlete. Apply the same energy and mental toughness that got you to this level when facing challenges at the next level.

Listed below is an exercise you can do to help you put things in perspective:

List five goals you want to accomplish:

1.
2.
3.
4.
5.

List five people you know from your professional team who can help you accomplish your goals:

1.
2.
3.
4.
5.

List five people you know personally who can help you accomplish your goals:

1.
2.
3.
4.
5.

List five characteristic traits you have that will be beneficial:

1.
2.
3.
4.
5.

List five transferable skills you have as an athlete:

1.
2.
3.
4.
5.

Now that you have identified your goals and transferable skills, you can use that as your baseline or foundation. That information will be valuable as you reimagine the new you in a different world.

CHAPTER TWELVE
Mental Toughness

"I have nothing in common with lazy people who blame others for their lack of success. Great things come from hard work and perseverance. No excuses."
—Kobe Bryant

As life evolves, there is yet to be a clear timeline for you to follow. The obstacles that arise may seem impossible to overcome. Pondering how to overcome those obstacles often leaves you perplexed and without a clear path. Michael Jordan once said, "Obstacles don't have to stop you. If you run into a wall, don't turn around and give up. Figure out how to climb it, go through it, or work around it." Find time to take a minute to reflect and put things in perspective as you move forward. Remember, "It's not about perfection. It is about being persistent and resilient, because your desire to succeed is too strong to be anything less." ~iriefitgirl. The adversity you face can come in many forms. The hustle may look different, but the struggle is the same, and how you overcome it is critical.

As an athlete, you are taught to think fast on your feet. And respond to the environment based on what is happening around you. You cannot always be in control, but you can learn how to pivot and adapt to what you are experiencing. I recall Karen Sutton saying, "Know your limitations and then defy them." Once again, being flexible is vital no matter who you are. If you succumb to your emotions, then you can potentially lose control and not accomplish anything - ultimately feeling like a failure. Be open to changing your goals based on your current situation. It is okay to reevaluate, adjust, take a step back, and revisit everything. Nothing is set in stone; the world is constantly evolving, like you.

Persistence and resilience are essential skills to have. When you are trying to reach a new level, your persistence gets you there. Timing is everything, and while you are playing, use this time to pursue the things you are passionate about. No need to overthink anything; take the risk, and have fun while you can. You heard the saying, "Proper preparation prevents poor performance." Think of this time as preparing to pivot to the future and take small steps until you reach your goal or goals. Having a sense of urgency in what you need even though you think you have a lot of time. Create a timeframe, so any challenges you face do not feel insurmountable. Any win, big or small, is a *win*. And remember to celebrate each win because you have made some progress. The only way to break down those barriers is by pushing through, no matter how hard it gets.

You do not have to conquer the world in one day. Instead, you can take one step or bite at a time, preventing you from overthinking and not moving forward. One day at a time will get you closer to your desired outcome. No matter what you go through, there is always a lesson behind it. The struggle is real - but not forever.

To thrive in a world full of demands and it is important to be resilient in different stages of the game we call life. Being resilient requires you to have the ability to recover or bounce back from some form of adversity, challenge, obstacle, or barrier. That obstacle usually comes when you feel defeated and like a failure, no matter your situation or internal or external pressure. Who can forget when Charles Barkley said, "If you are afraid of failure, you don't deserve to be successful." It is the challenge and mental toughness, *"Mamba Mentality,"* to learn from those mistakes or poor performance, even when you know failure is a part of the game of life.

As you think about your life choices and decisions, the best way to move forward is by letting go of things that do not represent or reflect who you are today. Even at this stage of the game, letting go of that old identity can be a struggle, referred to as a dichotomous identity. You do not have to let go of who you are, but accept that your circle will change as it should. Always keep in the back of your mind: every situation will require a different response and version of you based on the circumstances. As an athlete, being confident and committed to your goals show your resilience. Do not let it stop even when you fear the unknown in your business or personal life.

The best way to build resiliency is by exercising and learning coping strategies to manage stress, which requires you to know your stressors and rest. Self-awareness, perception, and a resilient mindset significantly influence your success.

Time is of the essence, so do not waste your energy on things considered distractors because, in the end, it will make you feel lost, depleted, helpless, and powerless. Instead, focus your energy on things you can control that will make you feel empowered and confident. Learn how to pivot from negative to positive thoughts and energy. That gives you a more positive outcome and outlook for your future. That should be motivation within itself.

The sky has no limits. It is up to you to shatter all expectations. What motivates you? Is it those intrinsic rewards such as being one of the best players on the team, the love of the sport and competitiveness, learning how to improve your performance, winning, or accomplishing your goals? Or extrinsic rewards, the things you control, such as being a team player, buying a new car, or that dream house? Motivation is the self-determination you have and cannot walk away from. Whatever it is, you are highly passionate about it. It is what you are willing to work hard for, no matter if you are tired, in pain, or stressed out; nothing will prevent you from getting it done. Now is the time if you still need to incorporate positive self-talk into your daily routine. That inner voice reinforces positive behaviors, motivation, and self-esteem. Positive self-talk reaffirms your beliefs and has a direct impact and influence on everything you do.

This is a quick recap on mindfulness because we often need a reminder about the importance of self-care and how we view things. I talked about mindfulness in one of the previous chapters. It is very powerful and vital to incorporate mindfulness into your day. It will change the game when you accept things or situations as they are. Do not make assumptions about anything. It will limit your ability as you move forward. Stay focused on the present and plan ahead. Mindfulness is using those guided images where you see your future self in the job you want or the lifestyle you will live. This technique can also be used when you are playing by limiting negative beliefs and decreasing anxiety. Mediation can be an option that allows you to focus on the task and not the outcome, reducing all distractions, not dwelling on mistakes, but shifting your focus to that present moment. Be flexible, try new things, adapt to your surroundings, stay engaged, and have fun.

It is essential to want to do something and stay committed to following it through. Motivation has a lot to do with your perception, attitude, and how you tackle each situation. It helps you shift from a can't to a can-do mindset when it pertains to you stepping outside of your comfort zone. You never know your influence on others and how you motivate them, so stay positive, be transparent, and authentic. Self-motivation is having grit, passion, and perseverance to achieve your long-term goals.

As you begin to leverage your platform and diligently work towards your future goals, it is essential to maintain that consistency, drive, and interest for the long haul. That is what you call grit. Grit is running a marathon even when you are faced with adversity, failure, and fear during the journey. You understand the barriers, but you continue to push through with courage. Everyone would have made it to the league if it was easy to be a professional athlete.

Ultimately, knowing where you are right now as a player is a means to an end. Therefore, you must keep all possibilities open while figuring out strategies to achieve all your goals, even when it seems impossible. But overall, it will be worth it. Commitment during this process is acknowledging you know and accepting the challenges that will come your way. A growth mindset will ensure you stick to whatever you are passionate about daily, monthly, or yearly. Once you acquire the growth mindset, you do not care how long your goals take because you know nothing happens overnight.

When you have grit and resilience, you learn to embrace challenges, setbacks, and criticisms while finding the light at the end of the tunnel. You often seek a path to master your skills and knowledge in an area of interest. You are determined to cross the finish line by any means necessary.

Defining your purpose and passion is needed when you have clear goals and work towards them daily. Mental toughness does not allow negative feedback or crazy hectic schedules to prevent you from moving forward. Humility is the knowledge that sometimes things will be hard, and you may not get the outcome you wanted or expected, but you're still grateful for the experience. You value the knowledge and lessons learned to give you the confidence to keep going. Finally, surround yourself with people who share the same vision and who can add value to you or you to them.

CONCLUSION

As we come to the end, I would first like to say, "*Thank You for reading my book!*" Over the years, my mission has been to help athletes who struggle with understanding the importance and magnitude of their platform, brand, and the impact on those around them. I know it is not easy walking into a situation where the world is watching your every move, and you feel like all eyes are on you. But, remember, this is bigger than you. The day you are drafted is the day you inherit this enormous responsibility, not only to you and your family but to your fans, to model the behaviors that will ultimately be a part of your legacy.

The practical strategies and tactical tools provided in this book will help you reevaluate and reimagine what the future you will look like. It highlights the steps you should start thinking about, or take, after you have processed and embraced the new identity you acquired once you entered the league. Considering it feels like being in the league will never end, especially in the first couple of years, the reality is nothing lasts forever, and you have to plan for the future at some point. The goal is for you to start planning sooner rather than later to hopefully eliminate some of the pitfalls others have made.

This may seem like an overwhelming process, especially when you start thinking about life beyond the game and the whole new identity you will take on. That is why taking small steps to lay the foundation and then build upon it is important. Like anything, stress and depression come when things stop abruptly and are out of control or when we are not prepared for the change we know is coming. So make sure to prepare.

Shifting the mindset is not easy but with practice, it becomes not only easier but a part of our daily habits. As you grow and learn, start exploring different opportunities. You only know what is out there if you start trying new things. Start working on those post-career goals and make them visible where you can see them often. Get a planner that will help you stay organized and map things out.

If you have found your dream job, work with a career coach who can help you identify those transferable skills and prepare you for the next business version of yourself.

Do not forget about your foundation and its impact on many underserved communities. There are many opportunities where your foundation can grow and flourish, such as mental health, education, or a group home, to name a few. Growing and sustaining your foundation can provide jobs for many in those communities. While you are helping the community, you also profit.

If you decide to be an entrepreneur, take a class on a topic that interests you. Having the right people on your team is essential, but be aware of what they tell you. That is called "*Common Mistake* 101." No, you will not know everything and will have to learn to trust those around you, but do not get completely caught off guard due to the lack of overall knowledge and have others talk around and/or overtop you. Take the time and invest in yourself! Trust me, the return investment on what you know will surpass any and everything else.

Embrace and accept the process! Do not act like change does not exist and is not coming. It is inevitable, and at some point, you must move forward. Utilize all the resources around you to make sound decisions that can position you to successfully pivot when you are ready to move from playing to life beyond the game.

Self-Care is a priority! Affirmations and mental mindfulness are a way of life. Do not be afraid to seek help from a professional if you need to. Your brain is the most important organ in your body, so protect it to ensure it is always working at the maximum and optimal level. Mental toughness is only as good as your brain's current state of mind. So be careful and gentle with it.

If you need assistance developing a blueprint consisting of a plan for where you are now and life beyond the game, consider working with my consultant company. The goal is to identify those transferable skills and align your vision with your current and future plans. Forward Movement Sports can help you with just that. It would be an honor to work with you on innovative and creative ways to leverage and monetize your platform and brand while making an impact and legacy for the future. Here's to the future you!

ACKNOWLEDGMENTS

Philippians 4: 13 states, "I can do all things through Christ who strengthens me." Thank you God for protecting me and providing me the opportunity to see my vision through. This has been a journey but one I had a lot of support to see completed. I could not have done this without my sons, Jaiden and Mekhi Williams. Because of them, I kept going. I am thankful for my little ones, Isiah and Amiyah Clark, for FaceTiming me, calling to make me laugh and smile and for hugs and kisses to keep me going. And also, my dog, Scott, kept me company by staying up late.

I am thankful for my sister, who is my biggest supporter and very proud of me. In addition, I am grateful for my cousin Vanessa Dawson who experienced a lot of this journey with me, and Angela "Minute" Dawson, who taught me to relax and stay focused. Also, thank you to my cousin Shawn Dawson, who drove me cross country to follow my dreams and Monica Morris for cheering me on.

I want to thank my Godmom Barbara Stokes-Hammond and Godbrother Darren "Butch" Stokes, for always being there for me. Special thank you to my late aunt Jean for always making me laugh. Thank you to my family and friends for keeping me in prayer.

ACKNOWLEDGMENTS

I am sending a special thanks to my friend, Na-im Blizzard, for his unwavering support and encouragement to keep going even when it was challenging to push through. Also, for constantly reminding me that I can do anything I set my mind to and follow my dreams because I deserve everything waiting for me. To be all I need and more without limits. To just have fun.

Grateful to my best friends and sister circle, Jannell Lewis-Johnson, Karen Williams, Nicole Grant, Tamara "Taj" George for being a part of my journey in sports, the long conversations, words of encouragement, and unlimited support. Thankful to Dr. David Clark for his ongoing support and time spent with my little ones. Thanks to JVonne Pearson for introducing me to Michael "Big Mike" Harris & Heavyweight Boxer Michael Grant who opened many doors for me. Grateful for John Welch for having enough energy to share when I was exhausted. Thank you, Dr. Arthur Wynn, for your support and pep talks since our doctoral program.

Special thank you to my NFL and NBA extended family Hollis Thomas, LaMar Campbell, Allen Aldridge Jr., Richard "Dirt" Jordan, Hugh Douglas, and LaMont Peterson for your support and answering all my questions.

I would be remiss not to mention Geo Derice for guiding me through this process until completion. He is one of the best book writing coaches. I appreciate all of the support he gave me. In addition, thank you, Dr. Nicoyla Williams, another book writing coach, for your writing sessions and ongoing feedback. Thank you, Tanya Hyman, for editing my book.

Thank you to the best mentors ever: Leah Wilcox, Que Gaskins, Walt Reeder Jr., and Carvin Haggins for paving the way for me to learn and grow. Thank you to all of the great athletes, sports administrators, journalists, commentators, coaches, and trainers from Chester, PA. It reminds me of a saying, "**What Chester Makes, Makes Chester**!"

ABOUT THE AUTHOR

Dr. Detra Johnson had a unique start in her career, beginning with the music industry, where she was the personal assistant to business mogul Troy Carter and the world-famous DJ Jazzy Jeff. These experiences taught Dr. Johnson about the music industry's business side, where she could network and cultivate positive relationships with top industry executives and artists. After leaving the industry, Dr. Johnson began working for Michael "Big Mike" Harris and continued to grow her network. Later she started her own company where she focused on public and community relations, marketing, and event planning for NFL, NBA, WNBA players, Professional Football Players Mothers Association (PFPMA), and entertainers.

After helping several of her clients transition from playing to life after the game, Dr. Johnson realized the best way to give back is to share her knowledge, experiences, and journeys with others. She believes you have to take risks to accomplish your goals. Her company, Forward Movement Sports Consultants, illuminates her vision through various programs that help youth - professional athletes develop their leadership skills, mental mindset, educational guidance, foundations, and transition from playing to life beyond the game.

ABOUT THE AUTHOR

Dr. Johnson is a graduate of Temple University and Wilmington University. Dr. Johnson holds a B.A. in Psychology, M.Ed. in School Leadership, and Ed.D. in Organizational Leadership, Learning, and Innovation. She is currently the Co-Chair of Community Relations for Black Sports Professionals Phoenix Chapter, a member of Women In Sports and Events, and an Associate Professor at Wilmington University, where she teaches multiple disciplines of Psychology and Organizational Leadership classes.

Made in the USA
Columbia, SC
06 December 2024